C000304133

An
Authentic
Servant

THE MARKS OF A
SPIRITUAL LEADER

Ajith Fernando

This booklet, edited and expanded by kind permission of the author, arose from an exposition he gave at the 1997 conference of Global Connections, UK.

Originally published by OMF International 1999. Reprinted 2001.

This revised and expanded edition 2006. Published jointly by the International Fellowship of Evangelical Students (IFES) and OMF International. All rights reserved.

Designed by Chris Gander
Printed in Singapore by Excel Print Media

An
Authentic
Servant

WHO WE ARE

In common with all evangelical agencies, the central purpose of OMF and IFES is to bring glory to God through building up his Church. To this end we work in partnership with churches locally and nationally.

OMF International was founded by James Hudson Taylor in 1865 as the China Inland Mission. The Fellowship's ministry began to extend across East Asia after the Communists came to power in China in 1949, and CIM missionaries gradually had to leave. 1,300 workers from 30 nations now serve the Church in East Asia, and share Christ's love with East Asian peoples worldwide. OMF's ministries are varied: evangelism and church planting, teaching, literature work, medical work, and placing Christians with professional skills, especially in countries where the majority religion is hostile to the Christian faith.

To receive our magazine *East Asia's Millions* (UK edition *East Asia's Billions*), or for news of OMF in your country, please go to www.omf.org

The International Fellowship of Evangelical Students (IFES) is working to proclaim the gospel of Christ in the world's universities. IFES is a Fellowship of national student movements in over 150 countries. Each shares the same doctrinal basis and the same aims, namely to equip students to be (i) effective evangelists; (ii) serious disciples; (iii) mission-minded Christians. There are still 18 countries with no known witness to Christ in their universities. IFES movements carry a range of names. Many English-speaking movements are known as FES; Russian-speaking movements as CCX; others as UCCF (UK); InterVarsity (US, Canada); TSCF (NZ).

To receive *Special Report* magazine, or for information on the IFES national movement in your country, please go to www.ifesworld.org

MORE IFES and OMF International have worked in partnership for many years. Almost all IFES movements in East Asia were pioneered by OMF missionaries, people whose faith had been nurtured in university Christian Unions. OMF continues to second staff to student ministry in East Asia, to serve with established IFES movements and to help pioneer new movements.

FOREWORD

The Apostle Paul's farewell to the Ephesian elders at Miletus (Acts 20:17-38) is deeply moving. Many leaders find themselves turning to this passage again and again. In v28 we read of how Paul urges the elders to keep watch over themselves, as well as the flock. Perhaps one of the truest indicators of our spiritual leadership is how we do that, and what we pray for ourselves. This booklet could be described as a commentary on that verse.

Spiritual leadership is a serious responsibility, and some carry that responsibility from their student years. Both of us had the privilege of leading a student Christian Union, and we trust this booklet will be used and talked about by student leaders now, as well as by church leaders, home group leaders, youth pastors, mission leaders...

In these few pages, Ajith Fernando cuts to the heart of the matter, raising critical questions often lost in our cultures of comfort. Are we willing for costly service? Do we yearn for those whom we lead? How can we keep our focus on the cross, and let the paradox of joy in suffering seep down into our understanding, our personal discipleship? There is no other authentic Christian leadership. Because of our fallen natures, and the pride which permeates all our attitudes and relationships, we are bound to struggle – and to find ourselves *constantly* struggling - if we are to win through to true servanthood.

We commend this booklet to you, and trust it will come as a great encouragement as you seek to live in Christ's service.

Patrick Fung
OMF International

Lindsay Brown
International Fellowship of Evangelical Students

*Paul wrote to the Christians in Corinth, 'Death is at
work in us, but life is at work in you.' In spiritual
ministry, we are called to die for the sake of others.
Are we willing for that?*

Even a superficial look at the New Testament would show
us that the cross of suffering is an essential part of
Christian ministry. We can safely say that if we try to get
round that, we will forfeit eternal fruitfulness. I think this is
an emphasis that has been neglected in contemporary
thinking about Christian service. We live in a society which
places much emphasis on comfort, convenience,
entertainment and good feelings. And because suffering is so
much at odds with this, we avoid it.

The lessons we draw here from the New Testament apply to
any spiritual leadership – in our churches, our missions, our
student fellowships. They are, in a sense, the marks of a
spiritual leader.

Being willing to die

Jesus said, 'Love each other as I have loved you' (John 15:12).
He explained how we do this, saying, 'Greater love has no
one than this, that he lay down his life for his friends' (John
15:13). Christians are people who are so committed to their
'friends' - those they minister among - that they lay down
their lives for them. This is the big divide between the kind
of commitment Jesus calls us to, and the world's
commitment. Jesus' description of the Good Shepherd in
John 10 shows this. When the wolf comes, the hired hand
abandons the sheep and runs away (vv 12,13). But the Good
Shepherd is different. He lays down his life for the sheep.

And we are to follow his example! When Christ died on the
cross, he paid the penalty for the sins of the whole world.
This is a price we finite and sinful individuals cannot pay. But
we are called to love 'one another', a smaller group than
everyone in the world. John 15:13 says Jesus died for his
friends. In the same way we, too, are to die for our friends.
This is a smaller group of people still, for whom we have
special responsibility - like our family, our congregation, and
the people we work with.

First among the friends we die for are our family members. Paul says 'Husbands, love your wives just as Christ loved the Church, and gave himself up for her' (Ephesians 5:25). Most wives would say, 'I don't want my husband to die for me. Just tell him to talk to me!' Talking when you are very tired is a kind of death. When we come back after a heavy day's ministry, and we are exhausted, we prefer not to talk. If there has been tension in the home, we know that if we bring the subject up it will lead to a conversation of an hour or two, so we avoid that. Part of our Christian commitment is to die to that desire not to talk.

So laying down our lives can mean many things. Most of us are not called literally to die for our friends. This example from family life shows that our calling may be subtler. We may be called to endure frustration, discomfort, tiredness and pain

laying down our lives can mean many things

because of others. That is not easy in this pragmatic age; society is so skilled at finding ways to avoid inconvenience.

Even Christians are swayed by the prevailing mood that gives prominence to convenience and ease. We, too, make our choices to avoid frustration, discomfort and pain. For example, when deciding where to serve, among our primary considerations could be the benefits offered like the salary, accommodation and pension. We hear people saying, 'I don't want to work in that country, because I don't like the climate.' When someone we work with becomes difficult, we just drop that person. When we find that those to whom we are called - the Muslims, for example, in a given area - persistently reject the gospel, we just leave and go somewhere more receptive. All this is alien to the basic call of Christ to discipleship. That was a call to deny ourselves, take up a cross and follow him (Mark 8:34). And a cross is a place where people die.

A theology of groaning

My basic premise is that when we are committed to the people we are called to serve, we will inevitably suffer pain. Let's see how Paul illustrated this principle. First note that he regarded groaning as an essential feature of life in a fallen world. This is a world subjected to frustration because of the fall (Romans 8:20). So even those who belong to God join the rest of creation in groaning. Of course for us this groaning is 'as in the pains of childbirth' - the groan of

Christians are people who can stay on

anticipation for those who look forward to a coming glory (Romans 8:22-23). 'Our present sufferings,' Paul says, 'are not worth comparing with the glory that will be revealed in us' (Romans 8:18). After listing a huge catalogue of trials, what did he say? 'We do not lose heart ... for our light and momentary troubles are achieving for us an eternal glory that far outweighs them all' (2 Corinthians 4:16-17). So we have a theology of groaning.

That heavenly vision enables us to groan with positive anticipation, and to stay on in difficult situations. I don't want to criticise people who leave difficult situations. God has called each of us to serve in different places, and there is no such thing as an easy situation for a disciple of Christ. But I think it is sad to see such a large number of Christians leaving situations of obvious conflict and hardship. Christians are people who can stay on in such situations because they are not afraid to groan. This is part of our theology. Because we groan with the joyous anticipation of glory, we are willing to live with frustration when our calling includes that.

Yearning for the lost

Once you have accepted groaning as an essential part of life, then you have the strength to yearn for people. We yearn firstly for the lost. Paul expresses this yearning in Romans 9:1-3, 'I have great sorrow and unceasing anguish in my heart. For I could wish that I myself were cursed and cut off from Christ, for the sake of my own race...' You can see how the yearning has produced hurt in him. As he contemplated the lostness of his own people he was broken up inside. Today people do all they can to avoid such pain. I believe this is one reason why so many Christians ignore or reject the doctrine of lostness of people outside Christ. They don't want to face the pain that such a doctrine will bring. Charles Spurgeon discusses those who say, 'I could not rest comfortably if I believed the orthodox doctrine about the ruin of men.' Spurgeon's response to this is: 'Most true. But what right have we to rest comfortably?'

So because yearning produces pain, people avoid yearning too. This yearning is a missing factor in ministry today. But it is yearning that produces urgency. Paul expresses this in 1 Corinthians 9:16: 'I am compelled to preach. Woe to me if I do not preach the gospel!' He was passionate for the gospel. The rest of this chapter expresses how that passion caused Paul to forfeit the rights of an apostle and to make so many adjustments to his lifestyle in order to reach as many people as possible. Imagine hearing this highly-educated Pharisee who was also a Roman citizen say, 'Though I am free and belong to no man, I make myself a slave to everyone to win as many as possible' (1 Corinthians 9:19). He climaxes this with the unforgettable words, 'I have become all things to all men so that by all possible means I might save some' (9:22).

Today we are afraid of such urgency. Perhaps some we have trusted and yearned for have hurt us. Perhaps projects that we earnestly gave ourselves to ended in

it is yearning that produces urgency

failure, resulting in disappointment and humiliation. So we don't want to break through that protective shield we have built around our emotions, because it makes us too vulnerable to pain. That's why we don't yearn for people with the urgency that Paul had.

There was a time when urgency was one of the things that attracted people to the gospel. It is said that Benjamin Franklin would go to hear George Whitefield preach because there before his eyes he could watch a person burn with passion. Today instead of urgency we have excellent programming, entertainment, and the promise of temporal blessings to attract people. In a generation dedicated to feeling good, we will avoid pain at all costs.

Yearning for believers

Just as we yearn for the lost until they come to Christ, we yearn for believers until Christ is formed in them. Using the vivid imagery of a woman in labour, Paul expresses this in Galatians 4:19: 'My dear children, for whom I am again in the pains of childbirth until Christ is formed in you, how I wish I could be with you and change my tone, because I am perplexed about you!' He identified so much with the Galatians that he hurt over their theological confusion.

he hurt over their theological confusion

We hear a lot of talk about incarnational ministry. But incarnation and pain are inseparable. When we cross the barrier from professionalism into yearning, we find that yearning brings hurting with it. I am surprised at how often people express relief over the breaking of some commitment they have. Maybe it is a difficult spouse or a difficult church, or difficult people. They move away from that spouse or church or those people, and save themselves from stress and pain. It is almost as if this liberation from pain or stress is seen as a sign of God's will in the decision. The biblical Christian accepts such pain as an essential part of commitment to people.

In 1 Thessalonians 2:8 Paul describes what lies behind that level of commitment. 'We loved you so much that we were delighted to share with you not only the gospel of God but our lives as well.' The verb translated 'loved you' is a very rare word. It doesn't occur often in the New Testament or in other Greek literature. It means 'we longed for you, or yearned for you'. Some translations have 'being affectionately desirous of you'. Paul goes on to talk of sharing 'not only the gospel of God, but our lives as well'. The word translated 'lives' is *psyche*, which means 'soul', or 'inner being'. Paul yearned for people so much that he opened his inner being to them. He had crossed from professionalism into yearning.

As a result of opening our lives in this way, we develop leaders. Paul describes how he opened his life to Timothy in 2 Timothy 3:10: 'You... know all about my teaching, my way of life, my purpose, faith, patience, love, endurance, persecutions, sufferings.' Through Paul's opening up Timothy knew all about him. So when Timothy went to Corinth, Paul was able to say, 'He will remind you of my way of life in Christ Jesus...' (1 Corinthians 4:17). If they want to know what he thinks and does, they should find out from Timothy.

Paul had reproduced himself by opening up, and developed Timothy and a host of other leaders.

Biblical stress

One of the results of opening our lives to others and yearning for them is stress. Paul described this in 2 Corinthians 11:28, 29: 'Besides everything else, I face daily the pressure of my concern for all the churches. Who is weak, and I do not feel weak? Who is led into sin, and I do not inwardly burn?' Today there is a lot of talk and many books about stress, and how to avoid it. I have found some of the books very helpful because often I take on stress for the wrong reasons.

driven people who find their primary fulfilment in success experience unbiblical stress

A lot of stress today is caused by not taking our Sabbath rest in this fast-paced society. Rest is an important aspect of the biblical lifestyle. Sometimes stress comes as a result of intense competitiveness. Driven people who find their primary fulfilment in success in this competitive society experience unbiblical stress because there is no guarantee of constant earthly success in this fallen world. Perhaps we suffer more than we dare admit from a 'Messiah complex' which makes us unwilling to delegate responsibilities to others. Thus we end up doing things that others could have done and bearing burdens which we should have shared with others. And we lose out on nurturing others, who would learn much from sharing our workload.

A lot of our stress, then, is unbiblical. Biblical stress comes out of a love for others, not a lust for achievement. It is the inevitable result of identifying so closely with people that we begin to bear their burdens.

7

Strength for taking on stress

If we are to take on biblical stress, we must first be strong enough to endure it. The strength for this comes from the joy of the Lord. There is an interesting sequence in John 15 which brings this out. In verses 12 and 13, Jesus gives his famous challenge to sacrificial love: 'Love each other as I have loved you. Greater love has no one than this: that he lay down his life for his friends.' But just before that he said, 'I have told you this so that my joy may be in you, and your joy may be complete' (John 15:11). In his letter to the Philippians, Paul too talked of lack of unity making joy incomplete (Philippians 2:2; 4:2).

Having the joy of the Lord in our lives is crucial. In fact I would say it is a requirement for effective ministry.

We will lose a lot of joy over things on earth because of the love we have for others. But there is one type of joy - the joy of the Lord - that we must ensure we keep. So Paul says in Philippians 4:4, 'Rejoice in the Lord always. I will say it again: Rejoice!' His repetition shows the importance of jealously guarding this joy.

we may have the stress of love, but we can't have the anxiety of unbelief

So how do we guard the joy of the Lord? Paul goes on to describe this. He begins, 'Let your gentleness be evident to all' (4:5). When the joy of the Lord is missing, gentleness goes, and we can become bitter about the way we have been treated in difficult situations. Then if provoked, we can react in an ungentle way. How, then, do we get this joy which will make us gentle? The answer is simple. 'Do not be anxious about anything' (4:6). We may have the stress of love, but we can't have the anxiety of unbelief. Now that is easy to say, but not so easy to achieve. Let's listen to Paul again: '...but in everything, by prayer and petition, with thanksgiving, present your requests to God' (Philippians 4:6). The 'but' here is a strong word (*alla* in the Greek). He is presenting an alternative course of action. In other words, we grapple with God in prayer until we have cast our burden on him. Then the burden is handed over to God. We are released from its power over us, and from our fear. Our joy is restored.

we grapple with God until joy and peace in believing return

The result is that the 'the peace of God, which transcends all understanding, will guard your hearts and your minds in Christ Jesus' (Philippians 4:7). This peace, like the joy of the Lord, is essential to life. Paul says it guards our hearts and minds. So we grapple with God until joy and peace in believing return. Only then can we go to a torn world and take on the stress we need to absorb if we are to be agents of God's healing.

Preserving joy

George Muller retired from running his orphanages at the age of 70, then spent 17 years as an itinerant evangelist. He was once asked the causes for such a long and happy life. He spoke of the joy he felt in God and in his work. The first great and primary business of each day was to have his soul happy in the Lord.

Grappling to preserve the joy of the Lord is a discipline we ought to cultivate. There is an example of this from the life of Hudson Taylor just after his first wife, Maria, died. Before he saw to the funeral arrangements, he went upstairs to his room and spent time alone with God. When it was time to close the coffin, he took one last look at his beloved wife, and again went up to his room to be alone with God. Only after this did he come back to complete the burial procedures.

John Stam of the China Inland Mission was shot along with his wife, Betty, by the Communists, when they were 29 and 30 years old. John once said, 'Take away everything I have, but do not take away the sweetness of walking and talking with the King of Glory'. The joy of the Lord was the one thing he could not be without.

God taught me this principle when I was having a hard time with my studies at university. I was doing a degree in biology, and it was a bad choice of subject as I am very weak with my hands. When doing dissections I would cut what I was supposed to leave, and leave behind what I was supposed to cut! And I can't draw at all. One third of our grade went for the practical lab work, and that was a disaster area for me. Besides, my heart was in the ministry, and I was longing to give my time for that. I often encountered depression and deep discouragement during those days. Later on I realised it had been a great privilege to be in that place. It was a Buddhist university with a vice-chancellor who was a Buddhist monk, and I was living in a Buddhist home. This, and the frustration of studying biology, was all part of my training for ministry. But it was difficult to go through at the time.

During this time I developed the discipline of walking, sometimes two or three miles, until I felt the joy of the Lord return. I had to come to grips with the situation, and let the belief in God's sovereignty break through into my life again. Only when this had happened would I turn back towards home. On the walk back, I would begin to intercede for others. But there was no intercession until the grappling with God was complete.

One of the greatest tragedies I see in ministry today is the number of angry Christian leaders there are who have lost their spiritual freshness. Sooner or later the weight of their anger shows in an ineffective and unattractive ministry. We must work at having our lives controlled by joy, not by anger. Angry people cannot be gentle under provocation. Any kind of provocation acts as a switch to release hidden anger. When we have joy in the Lord, however, the joy becomes our strength (Nehemiah 8:10). No earthly problem can take away that kind of joy. It becomes the most important thing in life, and we are able to remain strong because of it, in the midst of a crisis.

Sri Lanka is a country torn by strife between the Sinhala majority and the Tamil minority. We've also had a revolution by a group of Sinhala young people who tried to overthrow the government. There will be times when we have strong anger at what is happening, but that anger has to co-exist with the joy of the Lord. This came to a head for me in 1989. That year alone, we lost more than 50,000 people as a result of the Sinhala youth rebellion. There was never a time when there wasn't a dead body floating down the river at the edge of our city. And they were all young people. I knew some of those who died, and I was very angry.

The government set up a commission to inquire about why the young people were revolting. They asked interested people to make submissions to the commission. I felt this was a good time to express my

I soon realised that I was not handling my anger properly

outrage. We brought our staff together and prepared what turned out to be a very revolutionary document. We sent it to the commission. Some people who spoke out against the government at that time had been killed, including a leading journalist. After sending that document, I got up in the night a few times in a cold sweat, thinking they had come to take me. I felt it was my Christian responsibility to express this anger in a constructive way. But I soon realised that I was not handling my anger properly.

Many were leaving the country at this time, especially because of their children, as the schools were closed for long periods. My wife and I decided that whatever happened, we were not going to leave Sri Lanka. But wouldn't our children have a deprived upbringing? We concluded that if we kept a happy and contented home for our children, they would not be deprived in the ultimate sense. But my bad moods were not helping with this resolve. One day my wife said to the children so that I could hear, 'Father is in a bad mood. Let's hope he goes and reads his Bible.'

She had hit upon a very important theological truth. She knew that at this time when we were surrounded by anger, pain and death and the smell of bodies burning, we needed to spend time in the Word. Placed, as we were, in terrible temporal situations, we needed to expose ourselves to eternal truth and to focus on things that do not change. Then we would get strength, and with that strength joy would come: the joy that enables us to go out to the world and to take on the pain of other people. Another reason that George Müller gave for his long and happy life was the love he felt for the Scriptures and the constant recuperative power they exercised upon his whole being.

Moving from God to people

Christian ministers are people who get their strength from God. With his joy in our hearts, we will be able to take blows that come our way from angry people. If you hit the stomach of a strong person, he hardly feels it. If you hit a weak person, it can come like a hammer blow. We must become strong in this way by strengthening our spiritual muscles with the Lord's joy. This is essential if we are to be agents of reconciliation in this world. During a time of conflict in our ministry, the Lord taught me a very important principle: before you meet with people, first meet with God.

we get strength, then go and get bashed, get strength, go get bashed, get strength...

Our ministry springs primarily from God's acceptance of us.

I tell our staff in Youth for Christ that Christian ministers are those who first get their strength by being with God, and then go into the world to get bashed around. Then they come back, get strength from God, and go back into the world to get bashed around again. That is our life. We get strength, then we go and get bashed, get strength, go get bashed, get strength...

Motivation to ministry

A lot of talk about the possibility of serving in mission today focuses on excitement. It can result in people coming to serve who do not expect the suffering which will inevitably come. We must draw people in to Christian ministry by speaking of those unchanging truths; the truths which drove us to be involved in it. Foremost among these is the content of the gospel itself; the gospel of eternal salvation to those who accept it and eternal damnation to those who reject it. Such truths remain the same when there are problems and when things are going fine. When Christians come fired with a passion for people based on such awesome, unchanging truths, they will not give up or get disillusioned when the going gets tough.

Jesus motivated his disciples to missions in different ways at different times, including different aspects of the content of the gospel. For example Luke 24:46-47 says 'This is what is written: The Christ will suffer and rise from the dead on the third day, and repentance and forgiveness will be preached in his name to all nations.' The content of the gospel itself is always part of the Great Commission.

The great Scottish theologian, James Denney, once spoke at a missions conference, and almost his whole talk was on propitiation. Those who invited him were wondering what on earth he was up to, talking on propitiation at a missions conference. And just in his conclusion, he said that if propitiation is a reality then we must go and preach the gospel to the whole world. Let people see the horror of life without God and the glory of what the gospel can do to change that. Then they will be willing to face the cost of taking the gospel to people everywhere.

might the West soon disqualify itself from being a missionary-sending region?

So we focus on the great gospel, and we call people to be willing to die for it. Christians from affluent countries may be losing their ability to live with inconvenience, stress and hardship, as there is more and more emphasis on comfort and convenience. Many are unable to stick to their commitments when the going gets tough. They leave their places of service, change churches, and discard their friends. Some discard their spouses when their marriages face problems. What will this mean for the church in the West? Might the West soon disqualify itself from being a missionary-sending region? I think we are seeing some embarrassing examples.

I think we are seeing some embarrassing examples

Students often ask me, 'How can I prepare to be a missionary?' I usually answer by urging them to stick to the group they are part of, and to go through the pain of being there without giving up. That will make them skilled in facing the frustration and pain that is an unavoidable aspect of the missionary call. There is an unprecedented amount of study today on cultural anthropology and contextualisation, and I praise God for that. These studies are very helpful for incarnational ministry. But more helpful even than that is the ability to die, to die for those we are called to work with our families, our churches and our mission fields.

A doorway to disillusionment?

Sometimes when I present a challenge similar to what I have given above, sincere Christians fear that I may be encouraging people to live an unbalanced Christian life. They point to many who 'killed themselves' for the gospel and in the process neglected their health and their families. They are now very disillusioned as they struggle with physical and spiritual burnout, bitter spouses, rebellious children and a sense of defeat at the end of their ministries. Indeed it is important for us to look after our health as Christianity is concerned with the physical aspects of life too. But I think the Bible does leave room for situations where we will suffer physically owing to our commitment. Paul said, 'Though outwardly we are wasting away, yet inwardly we are being renewed day by day' (2 Corinthians 4:16). People who are being renewed inwardly will not end up disillusioned. Certainly disillusionment would not be God's will for his faithful servants.

How to live well, so we finish well

I believe that we would end our ministries well, and without disillusionment if, in addition to taking up the cross, we follow the other basic features of biblical discipleship. Let me summarise the features I've mentioned in this booklet:

- regular unhurried time with God in prayer and Bible study
- guarding the joy of the Lord
- taking our Sabbath rest
- working with the body by delegating responsibilities, and without trying to meet every need
- sacrificially fulfilling our responsibilities to our families
- looking forward to the coming glory which enables us to live with frustration on earth

f you neglect these features, don't even try to die for the cause of the gospel. You will suffer some sad consequences because of the neglect. If you take up these features, and others that obedience to Christ involves, you will be stretched to the fullest and often brought to the end of yourself, but God will see you through, and life will become a thrilling adventure. You will demonstrate through your life that 'the one who calls you is faithful and he will do it' (1 Thessalonians 5:24). Just after making his call to take up the cross, Jesus said, 'For whoever wants to save his life will lose it, but whoever loses his life for me and the gospel will save it' (Mark 8:35).

if you neglect these features, don't even try to die for the cause of the gospel

you have a serious calling and a high calling

God bless you as you seek to bring glory to the Lord Jesus Christ. You may be leading a large church, or a small Bible study group; you may be an elder or a youth worker; you may be an evangelist invited to speak on platforms, or you may be working to bring the light of Christ into a tough professional environment; you may be leading a mission agency, or leading a student fellowship on campus. In whatever place of influence God has set you, you have a serious calling and a high calling. May you finish well.

◆ ◆ ◆

STUDY QUESTIONS

The following questions were drawn up by Equip Ministries UK for use on their courses, after the first edition of this booklet appeared. We reproduce them here by kind permission.

Being willing to die

- In what ways do we see Christians working to avoid suffering? How have we done this ourselves?
- In your own ministry, what kind of things might 'laying down our lives' mean?
- How does the 'theology of groaning' help us to stay on in difficult situations? How can we encourage one another to look at spiritual ministry in this way?

Yearning for people

- Why do people avoid yearning for others?
- What would help us to feel greater urgency for the lost?
- What things do we long for in the lives of believers?
- What are the costs of opening up our lives to others?

Biblical stress

- What might be regarded as 'biblical stress'?
- What are some of the causes of stress in your ministry which could and should be avoided?

Preserving joy

- Do we perceive the joy of the Lord as a requirement for effective ministry? If we have already grasped this truth ourselves, how can we share it with other leaders? If we haven't, how can we re-align our ministry in this way? Are there other leaders we can talk and pray with?
- What lessons strike you from the illustrations in pp9-11?
- Are there circumstances in your life now in which the Lord may be teaching you similar lessons?
- How would you know if you had lost your spiritual freshness? Do you know the refreshing and recuperative power of the Scriptures?

Moving from God to people

- How do you get strength from God to withstand the blows?
- What unchanging truths motivate you for your ministry?
- What prevents us from becoming disillusioned?
- Of the basic features of discipleship on pp12-15, which would you be most in danger of neglecting?

JESUS DRIVEN MINISTRY by Ajith Fernando
IVP ISBN 978-0-85111-995-3 256pp
(USA Crossway ISBN 1-58134-445-7)

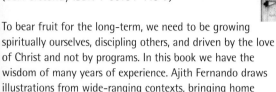

To bear fruit for the long-term, we need to be growing
spiritually ourselves, discipling others, and driven by the love
of Christ and not by programs. In this book we have the
wisdom of many years of experience. Ajith Fernando draws
illustrations from wide-ranging contexts, bringing home
biblical lessons in a warm and fresh way.

JESUS SAYS 'GO' by Robin Wells
Monarch/IFES/OMF/SIM ISBN 978-1-85424-730-8 160pp
(USA Monarch Books ISBN 978-0-8254-6114-9)

Are you thinking of short-term or long-term mission?
Here are searching questions with radical biblical
responses, and strong and colourful stories. The
'Interlude' includes contributions from John Stott,
Paul Borthwick and George Verwer. Rose Dowsett explains
how mission is in the character of God, and can be traced
right through the Bible. An unusual book.

Available from all Christian bookshops, or directly from
Inter-Varsity Press, Norton Street, Nottingham NG7 3HR, UK

UK
Trade order line: 0800 622968
Fax line: 0115 942 2694   Email: sales@ivpbooks.com

Rest of the world
Trade order line: +44 (0)115 978 1054
Fax line: +44 (0)115 942 2694
Email: international@ivpbooks.com

www.ivpbooks.com

ivp Inter-Varsity Press was founded in 1936 by
the then Inter-Varsity Fellowship (now UCCF).
It publishes Christian books which are true to the Bible and
which will communicate the gospel, develop discipleship and
strengthen the Church for its mission to the world.

*For a list of all OMF books on mission, and on the life of
faith, go to www.omf.org/books*

ALSO IN THIS FORMAT

THE GRACE OF GIVING by John Stott
IFES/Langham Partnership International
ISBN 978-1-899464-01-2

Ten principles of Christian giving from 2 Cor 8-9.
This booklet shows how regular giving is rooted in
three central themes of the gospel. It relates to
church giving, world mission, building projects, and relief
and development work. Pastoral and inspiring for Christians
at any stage.

MORE PRECIOUS THAN GOLD
Bible Reading Plan
IFES ISBN 1-899464-03-4

This plan, drawn up by Robert Murray McCheyne
(1813-1843), is used by Christians right across the
world. It goes through the New Testament and
Psalms twice and the rest of the Old Testament once, and
can be followed through a one-year or two-year cycle. Some
invite friends to work through it at the same time, to spur
each other on.

Available from any Christian bookshop or from
Inter-Varsity Press. Details on p17.